Cat Breeds

American Shorthairs

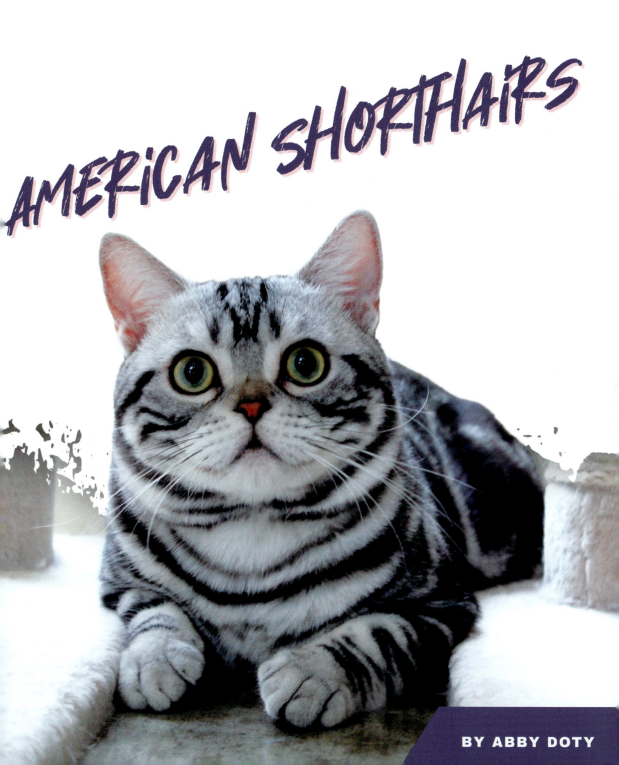

BY ABBY DOTY

WWW.APEXEDITIONS.COM

Copyright © 2025 by Apex Editions, Mendota Heights, MN 55120. All rights reserved. No part of this book may be reproduced or utilized in any form or by any means without written permission from the publisher.

Apex is distributed by North Star Editions:
sales@northstareditions.com | 888-417-0195

Produced for Apex by Red Line Editorial.

Photographs ©: Shutterstock Images, cover, 1, 4–5, 6–7, 8–9, 12, 13, 14–15, 16–17, 18–19, 20, 21, 22–23, 24–25, 26–27, 29; MPI/Archive Photos/Getty Images, 10–11

Library of Congress Control Number: 2024940540

ISBN
979-8-89250-306-8 (hardcover)
979-8-89250-344-0 (paperback)
979-8-89250-419-5 (ebook pdf)
979-8-89250-382-2 (hosted ebook)

Printed in the United States of America
Mankato, MN
012025

NOTE TO PARENTS AND EDUCATORS

Apex books are designed to build literacy skills in striving readers. Exciting, high-interest content attracts and holds readers' attention. The text is carefully leveled to allow students to achieve success quickly. Additional features, such as bolded glossary words for difficult terms, help build comprehension.

CHAPTER 1
PLAYFUL PETS 4

CHAPTER 2
MOUSE HUNTERS 10

CHAPTER 3
STRONG SHORTHAIRS 16

CHAPTER 4
CAT CARE 22

COMPREHENSION QUESTIONS • 28
GLOSSARY • 30
TO LEARN MORE • 31
ABOUT THE AUTHOR • 31
INDEX • 32

CHAPTER 1

PLAYFUL PETS

A silver American shorthair sits on top of a cat tree. Below, the family dog plays with a toy. The cat leaps from his perch to join.

American shorthairs often climb up high.

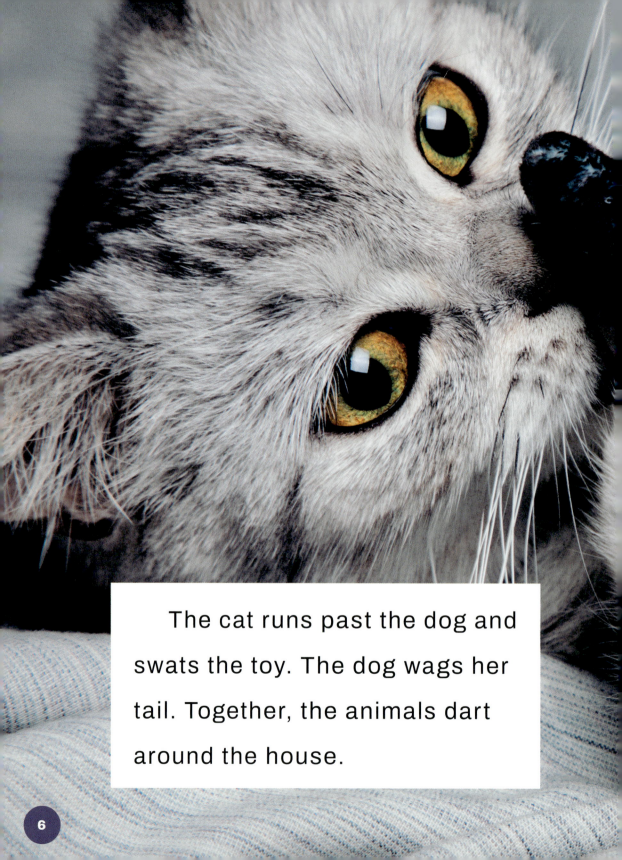

The cat runs past the dog and swats the toy. The dog wags her tail. Together, the animals dart around the house.

FAMILY PET

American shorthairs are friendly and gentle. The cats tend to get along with other pets. Playing with other animals can help American shorthairs stay active.

American shorthairs enjoy playing alone or with other animals.

A few minutes later, the cat sees a bird fly past the window. The cat jumps up to the sill and looks outside. He watches for more animals.

FAST FACT

Many house cats can jump up to 8 feet (2.4 m) high.

CHAPTER 2

MOUSE HUNTERS

European sailors used short-haired cats to catch **rodents** on ships. Some of these ships brought settlers across the Atlantic Ocean. By the early 1600s, many short-haired cats lived in North America.

Cats from British ships lived in Jamestown, a town built by settlers in North America.

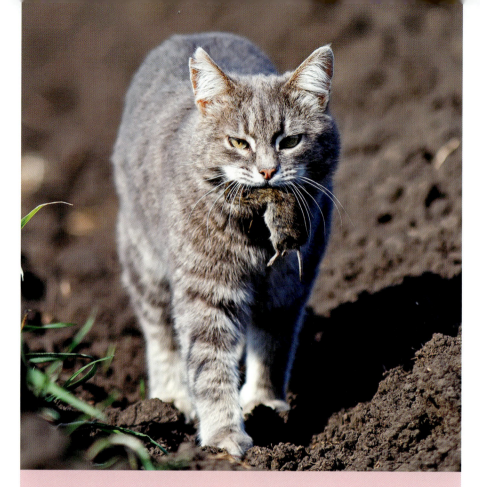

Many short-haired cats are good hunters. They stop rodents from eating plants or food.

In North America, the cats lived outside. They caught rodents around homes, businesses, and farms. By the late 1800s, people also kept the cats as pets.

CHANGES

Short-haired cats gained new **traits** over time. Some changes happened **naturally**. For example, the cats grew thicker fur. People caused other changes. They **bred** cats to have bigger heads and new fur colors.

Many short-haired cats lived in cold places. Thick fur helped them stay warm.

More and more people kept short-haired cats as pets. For a while, the cats were known as domestic shorthairs. In 1966, the **breed** started being called American shorthairs.

FAST FACT

A domestic shorthair was part of the first US cat show in 1895.

14

By the 2020s, American shorthairs were one of the most common cat breeds.

15

CHAPTER 3

STRONG SHORTHAIRS

American shorthairs are medium-sized cats. They have round faces and large eyes. Females weigh up to 12 pounds (5 kg). Males can weigh up to 15 pounds (7 kg).

Many American shorthairs have green or gold eyes.

American shorthairs have **stocky** bodies. Their legs are short and strong. Despite this **athletic** build, the cats have calm **personalities**.

WORKING CATS

American shorthairs were first kept to hunt rodents. So, the cats can run quickly. Many American shorthairs still try to chase prey. They may catch birds or bugs.

Most full-grown American shorthairs are 8 to 10 inches (20 to 25 cm) tall.

American shorthairs come in more than 80 colors and patterns. Silver tabby fur is common. Tabby coats can have a mix of swirls, stripes, and spots.

Cats with tabby coats have an M-shaped mark on their foreheads.

Many American shorthairs have reddish-brown coats.

FAST FACT

Some American shorthairs have calico coats. This pattern has three colors.

21

CHAPTER 4

Americans shorthairs' fur does not need a lot of care. Owners should try to brush their cats at least once a week.

American shorthairs shed most in spring and fall. They may need more brushing during these times.

Most American shorthairs should be fed two or three small meals each day.

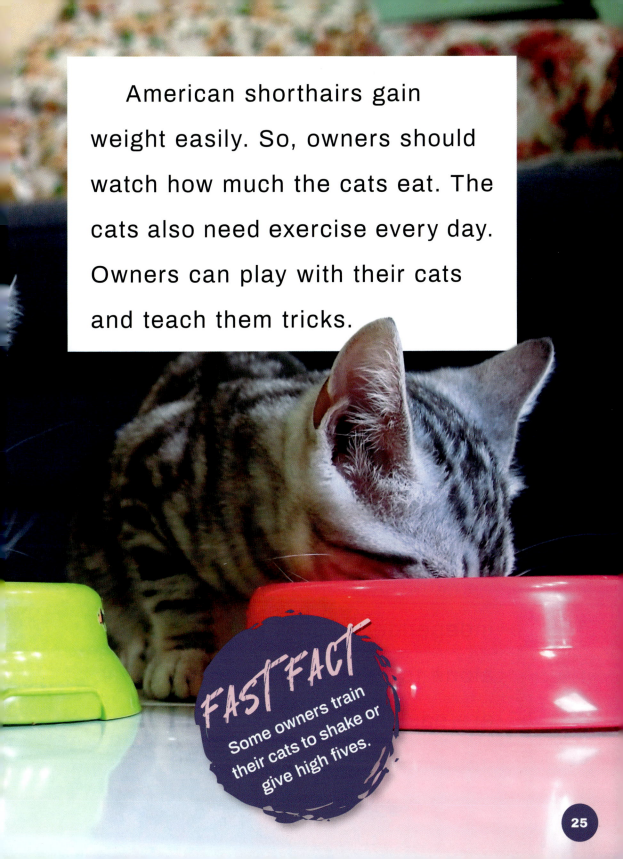

American shorthairs gain weight easily. So, owners should watch how much the cats eat. The cats also need exercise every day. Owners can play with their cats and teach them tricks.

FAST FACT

Some owners train their cats to shake or give high fives.

Many American shorthairs enjoy playing with children.

American shorthairs are independent. They can be left alone for several hours. And they are easy to care for. So, they are good cats for first-time owners.

NEW PEOPLE AND PLACES

Owners should **socialize** American shorthairs when the cats are young. People can take them to new settings. That helps the cats get used to being around unfamiliar places and people.

COMPREHENSION QUESTIONS

Write your answers on a separate piece of paper.

1. Write a few sentences explaining the main ideas of Chapter 2.

2. Would you like to own an American shorthair? Why or why not?

3. When did the American shorthair breed get its name?
   - A. the 1600s
   - B. 1895
   - C. 1966

4. How would playing with a cat help it avoid gaining weight?
   - A. Playing would make the cat eat more.
   - B. Playing would help the cat stay active and use more energy.
   - C. Playing would make the cat move less.

5. What does **prey** mean in this book?

*Many American shorthairs still try to chase **prey**. They may catch birds or bugs.*

    A. animals that eat other animals
    B. animals that swim in water
    C. animals that get eaten by other animals

6. What does **independent** mean in this book?

*American shorthairs are **independent**. They can be left alone for several hours.*

    A. able to be on their own
    B. needing to be watched all the time
    C. not friendly or calm

Answer key on page 32.

GLOSSARY

athletic
Showing speed, strength, or other active skills.

bred
Raised animals in a way that creates certain looks.

breed
A specific type of cat that has its own look and abilities.

naturally
Without being affected by humans.

personalities
The ways that people or animals usually act.

rodents
Small, furry animals with large front teeth, such as rats or mice.

socialize
To introduce a cat to new people, places, and things.

stocky
Wide and sturdy.

traits
Details that set animals apart from others, such as fur color or body shape.

TO LEARN MORE

BOOKS

Clausen-Grace, Nicki. *American Shorthairs*. Mankato, MN: Black Rabbit Books, 2020.

Jaycox, Jaclyn. *Read All About Cats*. North Mankato, MN: Capstone Publishing, 2021.

Pearson, Marie. *Cat Behavior*. Minneapolis: Abdo Publishing, 2024.

ONLINE RESOURCES

Visit **www.apexeditions.com** to find links and resources related to this title.

ABOUT THE AUTHOR

Abby Doty is a writer, editor, and booklover from Minnesota.

INDEX

A
Atlantic Ocean, 10

B
birds, 8, 18
breed, 14

C
calico, 21

D
dog, 4, 6
domestic shorthairs, 14

E
European, 10
exercise, 25

F
fur, 13, 20, 22

N
North America, 10, 12

P
prey, 18

R
rodents, 10, 12, 18

S
socialize, 27

T
tabby, 20
toy, 4, 6
traits, 13
tricks, 25

ANSWER KEY:
1. Answers will vary; 2. Answers will vary; 3. C; 4. B; 5. C; 6. A